STEP-UP
GEOGRAPHY

Local traffic - an environmental issue

Julia Roche

Evans

Published by Evans Brothers Limited
2A Portman Mansions
Chiltern Street
London W1U 6NR

© Evans Brothers Limited 2005

Produced for Evans Brothers Limited by
White-Thomson Publishing Ltd,
Bridgewater Business Centre,
210 High Street,
Lewes, East Sussex BN7 2NH

Printed in China by New Era Printing Co. Ltd

Project manager: Ruth Nason

Designer: Helen Nelson, Jet the Dog

Consultant: John Lace, School Improvement
Manager, Hampshire County Council

Cover: All photographs by Chris Fairclough

British Library Cataloguing in Publication Data

Roche, Julia

Local traffic : an environmental issue. - (Step-up
geography)

1.Urban transportation - Environmental aspects -
Juvenile literature 2.Local transit - Environmental
aspects - Juvenile literature

I. Title

388.4

ISBN: 0 237 528827

Special thanks to the following for their help and
involvement in the preparation of this book:
Coldean Primary School, Brighton, and St
Dominic's School, Harpenden.

Picture acknowledgements:

Corbis: pages 4t (Kim Sayer), 4b (E. O. Hoppé),
15 (Howard Davies); Chris Fairclough: pages 1, 5l,
6tr, 6cl, 6b, 7, 8t, 8b, 9b, 11t, 11b, 12, 13bl, 13br,
14, 16, 17, 19, 21t, 21b, 22t, 22c, 23, 24t, 24bl,
24br, 27; Chris Fairclough Photo Library: pages 5r,
6t, 9t, 26br; Michael Nason: pages 26l, 26cl;
Ordnance Survey: page 10 (Reproduced from
Ordnance Survey mapping on behalf of Her
Majesty's Stationery Office © 100043633 2004);
Geoff Webb: pages 18t, 18b; White-Thomson
Picture Library: pages 6br, 13t, 26t, 26cr.

Contents

Increased traffic **4**

Local solutions **6**

Visiting the site **8**

Deciding on the road's route **10**

Local people **12**

Having a say **14**

Points of view **16**

The changing landscape **18**

A questionnaire **20**

Democracy in action **22**

Reaching a decision **24**

Future traffic issues **26**

Glossary **28**

For teachers and parents **30**

Index **32**

Increased traffic

Traffic has become an important issue in Britain because of this country's density of population. Car ownership increases each year and roads become more crowded. This makes things difficult and dangerous for everyone, but especially for pedestrians and cyclists.

Try finding out about the beginnings of motorised traffic, when there were very few cars on our roads and they drove very slowly.

▲ *What towns do you know where there is busy traffic like this?*

◀ *This photograph was taken in the 1930s. It shows the same London street as the picture above.*

You could look for old photographs of the roads where you live and list all the differences you notice, compared with today. Look at the markings on the road and the street furniture, as well as the vehicles in which people are travelling.

Why are journeys made?

Journeys are made for a variety of reasons:

- travel to work, school, shopping, cinema and other entertainments, holidays;

- deliveries to shops and supermarkets;

- delivery of goods to our homes;

- emergencies requiring firefighters, police or ambulance.

Can you think of other reasons?

▼ *Traffic jams often occur where parents drive their children to and from school.*

How are journeys made?

Journeys can be made on foot, on a bicycle or motor bike, in cars, vans, lorries, buses, trains and, in some places, trams. For some journeys, motorised transport is essential: for example, delivering large quantities of goods to shops and supermarkets.

Make a list of the journeys you make in a typical day and how you travel. Could any of your journeys be made in a different way?

▲ *These children take a 'walking bus' to school. Like a real bus, it stops at set places on its route, at set times, so that children can join it at a stop near home.*

Local solutions

Many people are worried about traffic problems where they live. Local councils try to reduce the problems by making changes to the roads in their areas.

Have any of the following measures been introduced in your locality?

- cycle lanes;
- one-way streets;
- speed bumps;
- parking for people dropping children off at school;
- a pedestrian precinct;
- a bypass.

There is much discussion before measures like these are introduced. Some people may not be happy about the ideas and may wish to protest.

◀ Special lanes for buses or for bicycles help to make traffic flow more easily.

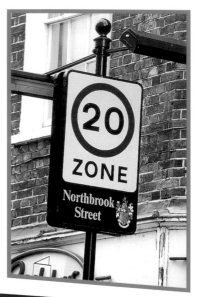

◀ Speed bumps and speed ▶ limits are designed to make local roads safer.

▶ The 'C's on this road in central London stand for 'congestion charge'. Drivers have to pay to enter this zone and this reduces the amount of traffic there.

◀ Pedestrianising parts of a town makes it more pleasant for many people, but not everyone is in favour of the measure.

Considering a bypass

Much of the traffic in many town centres is passing through on its way from one place to another. A bypass could be built to take this 'through traffic' around the edge of the town, and then there would be less traffic and fewer problems in the centre. However there are also arguments against building a bypass.

- **Cost**. Most of the money for road-building projects comes from central government, which gets its money from tax payers. Money spent on roads cannot be spent on other things, such as schools and hospitals, defence and police.

- **Environment**. Building a bypass takes up huge areas of land, usually greenfield sites, and so wildlife habitats and species of wild plants may be destroyed.

- **Pollution**. Traffic causes air, noise and light pollution. People living near the site of a proposed new road would be affected by extra pollution.

Can you think of other reasons why some people might protest about the building of a bypass? Try to find out more about the issues by reading articles in local newspapers or talking to friends or relatives who live in areas where a bypass is planned or being built.

On the map

Look at a road map of Britain and make a list of some cities, towns and villages, within a 50-mile radius of where you live, which have bypasses.

▲ A bypass is a main road, usually with four or six lanes, built to take through traffic around a city, town or other congested area.

Visiting the site

A good way of beginning to understand the issues involved in building a bypass, or any large building project, is to visit the site. This is called a field trip.

▼ *You might be able to visit a site where a bypass is planned or a site like this, where road-building is already underway.*

▶ *If you take photographs of the site with a digital camera, you can download them on a computer and use them in different ways for your work. E.g. enlarge, reduce, zoom in or out.*

What the site is like now

There are many ways of collecting information about what a place is like:

- Taking photographs.

- Using sound meters to measure sound levels at different places on the site and comparing your findings with those of other children.

- Drawing sketches of particular features of the site: e.g. machines uprooting trees and shrubs, or a wildlife pond being filled in.

- Tape-recording the sounds on site, such as workers' voices or machinery. Perhaps you could compare this recording with one made at a similar site where no work is underway.

- Making notes about any plants or animals which may be threatened once their habitat has disappeared.

▶ *If you visit a site before building work begins, you can investigate the wildlife that will be affected.*

Imagine

Think about road-builders with earth-moving machines beginning work on a site. They will be destroying the habitat of a creature or creatures. Look at it from the point of view of the animals, perhaps seeing the machines as predators, and needing to escape and search for a new home. Make notes and then write some prose or a poem on this subject. Try to use personification and powerful verbs in your writing.

After your field trip, use the data you have collected to draw sketches of how the site might have looked before work started and how it might look when it is finished.

9

Deciding on the road's route

Before the building of a road can begin, a huge amount of planning and research needs to be done. One of the most important issues to decide is the route that the road will take.

Where will the road be built?

If the purpose of the new road is to take traffic away from the town centre, then it must be built on land surrounding the town or village. This is usually farming land. The planners must negotiate to buy the necessary land from the landowners. This process can take a very long time.

Look at an Ordnance Survey (OS) map of your town or village to see where the bypass goes, if you have one, or where it might go if one was built.

▼ *What route would you suggest for a bypass for the village of Great Barford?*

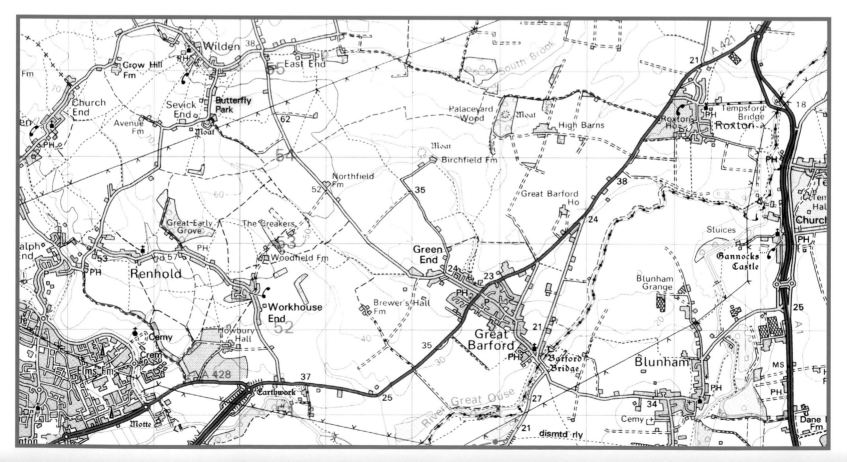

Changes to the landscape

The planners must think how they will make the road as safe as possible. They must consider the physical features of the area such as hills, valleys and rivers. They must also be aware of any places of special historic or scientific interest.

Where there are steep hills or mountains, the road must go through either a cutting or a tunnel. Sometimes an embankment must be built to carry the road over very low-lying land. This is done to avoid the risk of the road flooding in very wet weather. You can see symbols representing these features on OS maps. Roads raised in this way may become very noisy for people living nearby. Planners have to find ways of reducing this noise, perhaps by planting fast-growing trees and using high fencing.

Road tunnels

Two notable road tunnels are the Mont Blanc tunnel between France and Italy and the Laerdal-Aurland tunnel in Norway. Can you find them in an atlas? Which ranges of mountains do they pass through?

▲ *When you travel, see if you can notice fences, walls or trees by the roadside, designed to reduce traffic noise.*

▶ *These tubes stop animals from nibbling newly planted trees.*

Local people

People express many different opinions about the traffic problems where they live, and what they think the solutions could be. When a bypass is a possible solution, people will almost certainly join campaigns for and against the idea.

▶ *The opposing sides will have very good reasons for thinking as they do.*

Finding out what people think

Even if there are not plans to build a bypass where you live, there are probably plans to change the road system in some way: for example, to make a one-way system or put in new roundabouts or traffic lights. You will find that people have strong feelings about these.

The best way to find out what people think is to ask them. You might start with your family and friends or your neighbours, but discuss this with your parents before you go knocking on doors. You could, perhaps, go as an organised group to interview people in the high street.

◀ *Listen politely to people's opinions, even if you don't agree with them.*

Asking questions

Because people have strong feelings, their views may be one-sided. Your questions should be carefully worded and open-ended so that they encourage a balanced opinion. For example:

'What do you think would be one of the most important changes that could be made to this town with regard to traffic?'

'What do you think would be the advantages or disadvantages of a bypass?'

What might people say?

Prepare your questions beforehand and then discuss what you think some of the opinions might be. Afterwards, compare your predicted opinions with the results you get in your interviews.

Recording your results

Use a computer to record your results as a table, for example listing 'Points in favour of a bypass' and 'Points against a bypass'.

I live near where the bypass will be built and fear it will be very noisy and dusty.

A bypass would take traffic away from the town centre and less traffic means cleaner air.

The air we breathe

The air we breathe travels down into our lungs. Oxygen from that air is carried to every part of our bodies. Try to find out:

(1) How is oxygen carried round the body?

(2) Where in the human body are the lungs?

(3) Apart from oxygen, what else is in the air we breathe?

Having a say

It is important for everyone to take an interest in local issues, to make sure that any new projects in the locality are carried out in a way that is good for people now and in the future.

Expressing an opinion

We all express our points of view on many things, every day, in an informal way. You may have a school council through which you can express your opinions about school matters.

▼ *At a school council meeting, representatives from different classes bring forward the issues that concern the children in their class.*

Dear Sir,

I wish to express my strong opposition to the proposed new bypass.

People who live in this area have to travel 15 miles to the nearest hospital and not everyone has a car. The money that would be spent building a new road could be better spent on building a new hospital nearer to us.

A bypass would almost certainly bring more traffic round the town than we already have going through it, with a resulting increase in noise and air pollution and damage to health. There would then be an even greater need for access to hospital.

Yours faithfully,

▲ *Some people express their opinions on local issues by writing to the editor of their local paper. They hope that their letter will be published and read by many people.*

There are several ways for people to express their opinions on local issues:

- Writing a letter to the editor of the local newspaper.

- Attending public meetings and speaking at them. Going to the meetings is also a way of keeping up-to-date with the progress of planning for a project and the current facts and figures.

Many people protested about plans to cut down woodland, in order to make way for a bypass near Newbury. Some protesters lived in the trees, to try to stop the bypass going ahead.

Write a report

Write a newspaper report on a traffic issue, either an opinion piece or a balanced presentation of both sides of the story. Use publishing software to create the finished article.

Proving your point

You should back up your opinions with facts. For example, if you say that a road is dangerous, can you prove it by giving accident statistics or accounts of real-life experiences? By backing up your opinions, you may persuade people to agree with you.

Organisations that can help with statistics are:

- the police, at their local headquarters;
- the Department for Transport: www.dft.gov.uk;
- campaign groups such as Think Road Safety: www.thinkroadsafety.gov.uk.

- Organising demos (demonstrations) and protests. This is how some people draw attention to their opinions if they feel that they are not being listened to. Some demos are silent and this can be a powerful way of making a point.

- Contacting local radio or television programmes or even making a programme about the issue.

- Setting up a website.

Points of view

When a bypass is proposed, some people will think it is a good idea because it will reduce traffic and traffic accidents in the town. Some will be concerned about noise and damage to the environment, including wildlife habitats.

Try making some mind maps about the different points of view. Here is one about the advantages of a bypass.

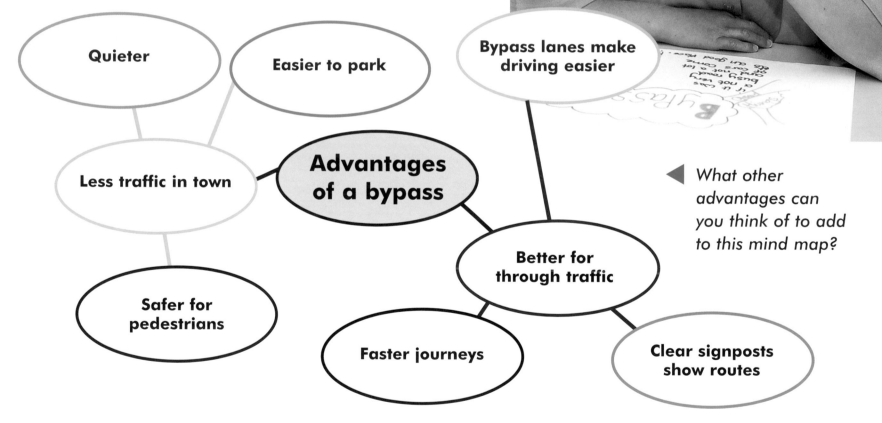

Quieter

Easier to park

Bypass lanes make driving easier

Less traffic in town

Advantages of a bypass

Safer for pedestrians

Better for through traffic

◀ *What other advantages can you think of to add to this mind map?*

Faster journeys

Clear signposts show routes

You could make a similar mind map about the disadvantages of building a bypass. You could include ideas about the road's impact on the environment and about the extra pollution that would be caused. For example, traffic on a new road causes noise pollution and light pollution. Vehicle exhaust pipes emit carbon dioxide and other greenhouse gases. The build-up of these gases in the air leads to global warming.

▲ *Some people worry that more roads will lead to more traffic, adding extra greenhouse gases, noise and artificial light to our environment.*

Internet research

Use the internet to find some other views. For example, you could visit the Friends of the Earth: Transport website (www.foe.co.uk/campaigns/transport). When using the websites of campaigning groups, remember that each has its own agenda or point of view, which influences the way in which it presents the facts.

Alternatives to new roads

Some people argue that, instead of building new roads, it would be better to find ways to reduce the number of car journeys people make. Try making a mind map about ways to reduce car traffic. You could include:

- encouraging greater use of bicycles;
- encouraging more use of public transport;
- introducing congestion charging;
- introducing park-and-ride schemes;
- building shops, schools and doctors' surgeries close to where people live.

The road planners' response

Protests about road-building projects have made road planners more aware of people's concerns about the environment. In most cases now, the road planners consider environmental issues very carefully at an early stage. This ensures that people have fewer objections to the plans. The plans can then be approved more easily and the road-building can begin more quickly.

Most road-building projects nowadays include plans for planting trees and shrubs and sowing wild flowers to replace the ones that the building work will destroy.

The changing landscape

All places change through time, but if plans to build a bypass go ahead, the area where it is built will change more quickly and dramatically.

If there is already a bypass around your town or village, or around a town or village near you, do you know what the area was like before the bypass was built? Your local history society and the public library will have old maps, photographs, newspapers and other documents to help you find out.

▲ *This railway line was closed down in the 1950s and the track became overgrown. A bypass built in the 1970s follows the route of the railway track at this point.*

◀ *This photograph was taken nearly 100 years ago. Today a bypass runs across the field behind the trees and there is a large roundabout here. Drainage was improved when the new road was built.*

How to find out about the past

Another good way to find out about the past is to talk to as many people as possible (family, friends and neighbours) who have lived in the area for quite a long time. With your parents' permission, you might try contacting some of the farmers who have their farms near the site of the bypass. There will be some interesting stories. Perhaps a bridge or underpass was built to allow the farmer to reach parts of his land which are now on the other side of the new road.

Contrasting descriptions

Think of adjectives to describe a bypass site (e.g. exciting, busy, noisy). Next think of some words to describe the area as it was before (e.g. green, tranquil, peaceful, with fresh air and birdsong).

Use the words you have collected to write two contrasting poems on the bypass theme.

Why local history is important

Knowing the story or history of our local area is important because:

- It is interesting to know how things were in earlier times.

- This knowledge helps us to respect what we have now and to plan well for the future.

▶ *You could take notes of what people tell you, or perhaps use a tape-recorder.*

Making a permanent record

We enjoy and benefit from looking back at records of changes in our landscape which have happened throughout history. Perhaps you can find a way to make a permanent record of changes that are happening near you now, for people in the future to enjoy.

A questionnaire

Open-ended questions, like those you thought about on page 13, encourage people to give their ideas and opinions. By contrast, the questions in a questionnaire are designed so that everyone can choose one out of several simple answers.

In some questionnaires, people are asked to answer each question by ticking 'yes', 'no' or 'don't know'. In others, they are asked to pick the answer that they most agree with. For example:

Do you like playing football?

❑ Yes, very much

❑ Yes, quite a lot

❑ No, not much

❑ No, definitely not

How often do you cycle to school?

A   Every day
B   More than twice a week
C   Once a week
D   Less often than that
E   Never

People's answers to questions like these can be counted and recorded in a graphical way, such as a block graph or pie chart.

Feelings about football

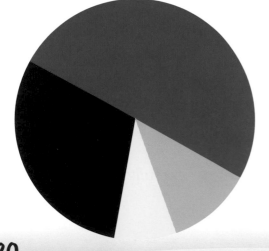

◀ *This pie chart shows that 50 per cent of the people asked said that they definitely do not like football.*

▶ *Try turning the results shown in this bar graph into percentages.*

Frequency of cycling to school

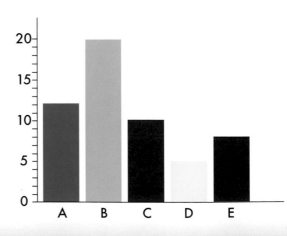

The results of a questionnaire can help people to make a decision. For example, if 90 per cent of children said that they never cycled to school, the school might decide not to build a new bike shed. However, the children might say that they would cycle to school if there were bike sheds there.

Preparing a questionnaire

In a group, think of a list of key questions to include in a questionnaire about a proposal to build a bypass. When you first try this, you may find that many of the questions you think of are the same as each other but just expressed differently. Choose your questions carefully to avoid repetition.

▲ Make sure that all your questions can be answered by a 'YES', 'NO' or 'DON'T KNOW'. This will make it easier for you to count your results.

If you compose your questions on the computer, you will find it easy to reword them and add new ones or take away the ones you do not want. You can also print multiple copies.

◀ Check your questionnaire carefully before you print out lots of copies.

Democracy in action

Our society is based on a system called democracy. In a democracy, everyone has the right to express their point of view. When all who wish to have given their opinion, a vote is taken and everyone accepts the decision of the majority. Do you sometimes make a class decision, by seeing how the majority vote?

▲
◄ Think about methods of making decisions that you use with your friends. How do they work? Are they fair to everyone?

Elections

In a democratic country, adults can vote in elections to choose the people who will represent them in their local council or in the national parliament. Usually, the people who stand for election as councillors or members of parliament belong to a political party.

▲ At election times, political parties produce leaflets about their ideas, which are delivered to people's homes. Take time to look at some of these and see what they say about plans to reduce traffic problems.

Listening to public opinion

The people who are elected to a council or to parliament want to please the majority so that they will be re-elected in the future. Therefore they listen carefully to public opinion.

A public meeting

When a change like a bypass is proposed, a council may hold a public meeting. It is important that everyone's opinion is heard and respected, before any decision is made.

Perhaps you could organise a public meeting in class to discuss a proposal for a bypass. Everyone should take on a different role, such as a local delivery driver, a Friends of the Earth campaigner, a firefighter or a resident who lives near the site of the bypass. Everyone should have an opportunity to be listened to politely.

You should be confident about your opinion before you start, but be prepared to change your mind if you hear a convincing argument.

Use a variety of methods, such as an overhead projector or interactive whiteboard, to display any data you have collected to back up your points.

Presentation

For display at the 'public meeting', create a Power Point presentation using digital photos and written descriptions of the bypass, together with graphs and pie charts of the data you have collected.

cars	37
motor bikes	9
buses	10
vans	26
lorries	19
other	13

▶ *Use graphs and other images to help you make your point.*

Reaching a decision

Just as you have been doing, when a bypass is proposed, a local council must look at all the issues and find out about public opinion. The council must also investigate the cost of the proposals. Finally, a decision must be made.

Which issues are the most important?

You have tried to look at the issues from the points of view of many different people. Which issues were spoken about most frequently during your 'public meeting' (page 23)? Make a list of four or five of them.

▲ *You will need to count the answers people have given on your questionnaires. Be careful to count them accurately.*

People wanted less traffic in the town centre, but they also wanted to be able to drive to the shops.

Many people mentioned health. They said that we would have cleaner air and more exercise if we used our cars less.

Use the data collected from your questionnaires (page 21). Which issues collected the greatest number of 'yes's or 'no's? List the top four or five.

▶ *When you have counted how many people have answered 'yes' and 'no' to each question, you can turn the results into percentages.*

Change the plans or scrap the bypass?

Now that you have a clearer idea of what the main issues are, it is time to think about whether or not a bypass is the best solution to traffic problems in the town.

Your questionnaires may have shown that many people are in favour of a new road as shown in the plans.

Some may have agreed that there should be a bypass but think that it should take a different route.

Others may feel strongly that building a bypass is not the right way to deal with the traffic problems in the town or village and that the plans should be scrapped.

	LOCAL TRAFFIC QUESTIONNAIRE			
	QUESTION	YES	NO	DON'T KNOW
1	Do you think we have traffic problems in our town?	✓		
2	Do you think there is too much traffic in the High Street?	✓		
3	Do you worry about fumes polluting the air?	✓		
4	Do you think a new bypass would be a good solution to the problems?		✓	
5	Would you worry about the cost of a new bypass?	✓		
6	Would you worry about the destruction of plant/wildlife habitats?	✓		
7	Would you worry about noise pollution during and after construction?	✓		
8	Do you think the money spent on a bypass could be better spent differently?	✓		
9	If 'yes' would you choose: hospital Sport and leisure Public transport?	....✓..		
10	Do you live in the High Street?		✓	

A letter to the council

Use your findings to compose a letter to the council to persuade them to agree with your majority view. Make all your points clearly and politely, backing up each statement with facts and figures. For example:

'43% of those interviewed said …'

'Statistics from a similar area where a bypass was built show a 10% increase in cases of asthma in the 5 years since the road opened.'

Future traffic issues

The problems associated with motorised traffic will continue well into the future and will become worse unless big changes are made.

Building new roads may solve the immediate problems in towns and villages but statistics show that, as more roads are built, the amount of traffic increases. The number of accidents falls in some towns and villages when a bypass is built, but more traffic, travelling faster, brings an increase in noise and air pollution and, as a result, global warming.

▲
◄ *Trams and trains are more environmentally friendly than cars.*

► *Roads with cycle lanes encourage more people to travel by bike. Cycling does no harm to the environment and is a good way of keeping fit.*

Welcome to Cambridge park&ride

- ● **Cowley Road**
- ● Grafton Centre
- ● City Centre
- ● Addenbrooke's
- ● Babraham Road

Route 99 Departs :- Monday to Sa
from 06.25 every 10 minutes until 18.45 (6.45) then every 20 minutes
Last bus from the City 20.30 (8.30pm)

All buses serve the Historic City Centre and the Grafton Centre
*Please note that at peak times some journeys stop at Short Street for the Grafton Centre

FREE PARKING

Return Fare to the City
£1·80 PER PERSON
THREE CHILDREN UNDER 15 TRAVEL FREE
WITH EACH FARE PAYING ADULT

PLEASE PAY ON THE BUS

MEGARIDER 7 DAYS £8.50 · DAYRIDER **£3.00 Unlimited Travel**

Stagecoach in Cambridge

travetine

Cambridgeshire County Council

Park and Ride is a quality partnership between Cambridgeshire County Council, Cambridge City Council and Stagecoach

▲ *A park-and-ride scheme can help reduce traffic in a town centre. Large car parks are provided on the outskirts of the town, and there are regular buses from there to the centre.*

Design a leaflet

Design a leaflet to encourage people to think about reducing their use of cars. Illustrate the benefits to air quality, health and also energy saving.

Our travel choices

The travel choices we make depend on a number of things:

- Whether we live in urban areas with good public transport or rural areas where public transport is less available.

- The distance we have to travel.

- Whether we travel alone or have a family or equipment to transport.

- The time a journey will take using one form of transport rather than another.

A delivery driver carrying goods to shops has no choice but to use his firm's lorry, truck or van. Think about how each member of your family travels at the moment, for any of the journeys you have to make. Use the computer to make a list of how you travel now and how you might travel in more environmentally friendly ways.

Sustainable approaches

We must think seriously about how we can have convenient methods of transport and, at the same time, reduce the damage being done to the environment. We must:

- Reduce petrol fume emissions from all vehicles. Scientists are constantly working to find cleaner fuels.

- Be willing to try new ways of travelling: e.g. electric cars, or the yellow bus for school journeys, if it comes to your area.

▶ *Have a class discussion about different ways of coming to school.*

My dad says I can cycle to school when I have passed my cycling proficiency test.

I walk to school except when the nights get darker.

27

Glossary

agenda — a list of things to be done.

argument — a reason put forward to support a point of view.

asthma — a breathing disorder often caused by an allergy. It involves wheezing and a tight feeling in the chest.

campaign — a series of organised activities, such as public speaking and demonstrations, designed to gain supporters for a proposal.

central government — the elected representatives (members of parliament) who meet at the House of Commons in London, to make decisions about running the country.

congested — crowded.

congestion charge — a fee that drivers must pay to enter a certain area. The purpose is to discourage drivers from entering an area where traffic tends to be very heavy.

council — the group of people who are elected by local people to run a town or village.

current — happening now.

cutting — an excavation through a piece of high land for a road or railway to pass through without changing level.

data — information in the form of measurements, facts or observations.

democracy — government by the people or by their elected representatives. The word comes from the Greek *demos* (people) and *kratos* (power).

demos — an abbreviation of 'demonstrations': meetings, marches and other actions by which people show that they are protesting about something.

density of population — the number of people living in a specific area. In the UK, the average population density is 242 people per square kilometre.

election — the act of choosing the people who will represent us on different committees, councils or in parliament.

embankment — a man-made ridge of earth or stone that carries a road or railway.

environment — the surroundings in which people, plants or animals live, or in which people work.

global warming — gradual warming of the earth's atmosphere caused by an increase in carbon dioxide and other air pollution which traps in heat.

greenfield sites — areas of the country which have not previously been built on.

habitats — the natural homes of animals or plants.

impact — effect.

locality — your own local area or the area around a particular building or site.

majority	the largest group sharing one opinion when a decision is made.
mind map	a diagram, also known as a spidergram, which shows related thoughts. You write the main subject or question in the centre, and then write all your ideas about this, at the end of lines drawn from it.
motorised	having a motor.
multiple	more than one (usually many).
negotiate	to work or talk with others to reach an agreement.
notable	worthy of being noticed or remembered.
open-ended	cannot be answered with a 'yes' or 'no' and encourages people to talk more about a subject.
Ordnance Survey	Britain's national mapping agency, which makes very detailed maps of every area of Great Britain.
park-and-ride	a system where drivers park away from the town centre and take a bus from the car park to the town centre.
parliament	the highest law-making authority in Britain, made up of the House of Commons, the House of Lords and the sovereign (the present king or queen).
physical features	the natural parts that make up the earth's surface, e.g. mountains, rivers and seas.
proposal	a suggested plan which is being put forward for consideration by a committee or council.

radius	the distance from the centre of a circle to its circumference. 'Within a radius of 50 miles from your home' means less than 50 miles from your home, in any direction. Imagine your home as the centre of a circle, with a radius of 50 miles.
research	investigating the facts about a subject.
rural	in the country.
species	types of plants and animals.
street furniture	signposts, lamp posts, benches, and all other objects like these that are added to our streets.
tax payers	people who earn wages or salaries by working. They must, by law, pay some of their earnings as taxes to the government, who use it to pay for defence of the country (army, air force and navy), schools, hospitals, the police, fire service, road building and many other important things that we need.
urban	in towns.
walking bus	a way for children to walk safely to school. Each day at the same time, known adults walk along the same route, so that children can join them at a set place.
yellow bus	bus put on specially to take children from near their homes to school, and back again at the end of the day. Yellow bus schemes are an idea taken from the USA, where all school buses are yellow.

For teachers and parents

This book is designed to support and extend the learning objectives of Unit 20 of the QCA Geography Scheme of Work.

As they use the book, the children are encouraged to explore issues including 'Should we build more roads or develop those we have, in different ways?' During this work they will investigate a variety of environmental topics and issues of land use and also learn about the democratic process used to make local decisions. The aim is that the children will increase their ability to:

- Observe and question
- Collect and record evidence
- Use maps and plans
- Use secondary sources
- Undertake fieldwork
- Appreciate the quality of an environment
- Use ICT to access and to present information
- Communicate and explain issues
- Understand different viewpoints

SUGGESTED FURTHER ACTIVITIES

Pages 4-5 Increased traffic
Some further work on this theme could, very probably, begin at the school gates. Children could be asked to canvass opinion from their parents or guardians about the traffic situation at the beginning and end of each school day. Later, in discussion, the children might be able to suggest some ways of improving the situation. Visit www.sustrans.com for some more ideas.

This page would also lend itself nicely to a history follow-up. See http://www.3wheelers.com/history.html for an interesting timeline. In 1865 the Road and Locomotives Highway Act required a person to walk in front of a vehicle, waving a red flag to warn others of the vehicle's presence. The act set speed limits of 2mph in towns and 4mph in the country. Ask the children to try to find out the average speed of a cyclist.

Pages 6-7 Local solutions
http://www.cclondon.com explains the reasons for congestion charging and provides a journey planner offering alternative methods of travelling.

You might like to do some work on the pros and cons of cars versus public transport.

This book, like Unit 20 of the Scheme of Work, focuses on the example of building a bypass; but the processes suggested for investigating this subject can be applied to any local traffic or road improvement scheme.

Pages 8-9 Visiting the site
You might do some work on plants and animals which would be affected if a bypass was built. www.wildfile.co.uk has lots of links for information and activities. After some research with the children you might have a discussion about why conservation is important. You will find some starting points for this in another book in this series, WHAT'S IN THE NEWS? page 20.

www.protectourwoodland.fsnet.co.uk has a good exposition of problems in Worthing. There is a section on the parish and town councillors' role in planning, as well as discussion of the responsibilities of the councillors and ourselves either as residents or as visitors.

Pages 10-11 Deciding on the road's route
The proposed bypass for Great Barford runs north of the village, from the A428/A421 junction to the A1/A421 junction.

If there was an opportunity, the children could do some design and technology by building their own model of a stretch of bypass. You could use the picture on page 11 as a starting point and add as much or as little detail as you have time for. Fences and trees would be important with the wrapping on the lower part of each tree trunk to protect it from animals nibbling. Some children could arrange lighting and barriers along the central reservation.

Another possible avenue for study would be the problem of flooding and what strategies are being used to reduce the dangers. The issue of building on flood plains might be one to explore. Go to http://www.environment-agency.gov.uk/subjects/flood and click on 'What does the Foresight report show?'

Or go to http://www.english-nature.org.uk and select 'Nature for Schools' > 'Primary resources' > 'Traffic, the Environment and Me'. This site contains a wealth of material including lesson notes, background information including SSSIs, statistics about pollution and health, travel options and age-related activities including some ideas for role play.

Pages 12-13 Local people

If and when traffic is taken away from the high street, it will certainly be safer and quieter but what impact will this have on shopkeepers? Ask the children to prepare some ideas, perhaps at home, and then discuss them in class.

Pages 14-15 Having a say

To help with backing up opinions with facts, www.thinkroadsafety.gov.uk has a catalogue of posters and publications, advice for cyclists and roller-bladers and lots of excellent information for parents and teachers.

Pages 16-17 Points of view

Discuss the issue of bias in reports and stories. You might ask the children to rewrite the story of Red Riding Hood from the viewpoint of either Red Riding Hood or the wolf. The stories could then be compared. Comparing the same story in a variety of newspapers could also be helpful in this context.

Pages 18-19 The changing landscape

Your local history society or the archives and local studies department of your main library might agree to send someone along to talk to the children about local issues:

■ changing road layouts
■ growth of traffic
■ growth of population and development of the town or village.

They will also have useful resources such as photographs and maps to show the children.

Pages 20-21 A questionnaire

To extend the work on percentages, you might like to do some work with the children on comparing vulgar fractions, decimal fractions and percentages, using a set of data collected by the children or a set made up to suit the page.

If you want to use real data and a larger sample, you might involve some other classes.

Pages 22-23 Democracy in action

This would be a good opportunity to introduce some work on how our country is governed. To use as a stimulus, you might video-record a session of 'Question time' in the House of Commons or, even better, the events on the day of the State Opening of Parliament in November, and select parts of it to show the children. Lots of excellent work could be done relating to citizenship and history, such as:

■ How do people become members of the House of Lords/House of Commons?

■ How do ordinary people make their voices heard in our democratic country?

■ What is a debate and how does it work?

For teachers' resources, news, games, tour of the palace of Westminster and glossary of parliamentary vocabulary, visit: http://www.parliament.uk and click on 'Explore Parliament', which is a separate site run by the Parliamentary Educational Unit.

Pages 24-25 Reaching a decision

Now that the children have some idea of how a debate works, perhaps you could organise one in class to discuss one of the issues where opinions seem divided. Help the children to compose a motion and discuss the rules. You could perhaps create a more orderly model than that of the actual House of Commons.

Pages 26-27 Future traffic issues

The children could visit www.youngtransnet.org.uk, a site which helps young people with transport research and action.

The children could use a map of the British Isles to identify a city, some distance from home, that they would like to visit, plan their journey there (a) by car and (b) by train, and decide which they would choose. They should use a road map or the internet (e.g. www.greenflag.co.uk/routeplanning/index.asp) to plan the car journey and work out the journey time, with adult help. www.nationalrail.co.uk/planmyjourney will help them plan the train journey.

Some road safety work could be included here with time being given to studying and discussing the sections of the Highway Code relating to pedestrians and cyclists. The children could, perhaps, make their own copy of the relevant rules with illustrations for display in the classroom and more widely round the school. They might be used first as stimulus for an assembly.

Discuss the possibility of children attending cycling proficiency courses.

Index

accidents 15, 16, 26
air 13, 16, 24
air pollution 7, 16, 26
ambulance 5
animals 9, 11

bicycles 5, 6, 17, 26 (see
    also cyclists)
block graph 20
bridge 19
buses 5, 6, 26
    yellow buses 27
bus lane 6
bypass 6, 7, 8, 10, 12,
    15, 18, 19, 23, 24, 26
    advantages and
        disadvantages 13, 16
    proposed 14, 16, 21,
        23, 24-25
    route 10

campaign groups 15, 17
campaigns 12
carbon dioxide 16
cars 4, 5, 14, 17, 24, 26
    electric cars 27
congestion charge 6, 17
councils 6, 22, 23, 24, 25
cuttings 11
cycle lanes 6, 26
cyclists 4, 20, 21, 27

decisions 22, 23, 24
deliveries 5
delivery drivers 23, 27
democracy 22
demos (demonstrations)
    15

Department for Transport
    15
drainage 18

earth-moving machines
    9
elections 22
embankments 11
emergencies 5
energy saving 26
environment 7, 16, 17,
    26, 27

farmers 19
fencing 11
field trip 8, 9
firefighters 5, 23
flooding 11
Friends of the Earth 17,
    23

global warming 16, 26
government 7
Great Barford 10
greenfield sites 7
greenhouse gases 16, 17

habitats 7, 9, 16
health 14, 24, 26
history, local 18, 19
hospitals 7, 14

journeys
    car 17
    methods of travel 5, 27
    reasons for 5

land 7, 10, 11, 19

light pollution 7, 16, 17

majority 22, 23
maps
    old 18
    Ordnance Survey 10,
        11
    road 7
meetings, public 14, 23,
    24
mind maps 16, 17
mountains 11

Newbury 15
newspapers, local 7, 14
noise 7, 11, 14, 16, 17,
    26

one-way streets 6, 12
opinions 12, 13, 14, 15,
    20, 22, 23
oxygen 13

park-and-ride 17, 26
parking 6
parliament 22, 23
pedestrian precinct 6
pedestrians 4, 16
percentages 20, 25
photographs
    old 4, 18
    taking 8, 9
pie charts 20, 23
plants 7, 9
police 5, 7, 15
political parties 22
pollution 7, 14, 16
population density 4

protest 6, 7, 15
public opinion 23, 24
public transport 17, 27

questionnaires 20-21, 24,
    25
questions, open-ended
    13, 20

railway 18
road-building 7, 8, 9, 10,
    17
road markings 4
roads 4, 6, 7, 10, 11, 12,
    14, 16, 17, 26
roundabouts 12, 18

school council 14
schools 5, 6, 7, 17, 27
shops 5, 17, 24, 27
signposts 16
speed bumps 6
speed limits 6
statistics 15, 25, 26
street furniture 4

tax payer 7
Think Road Safety 15
traffic lights 12
trains 5, 26
trams 5, 26
trees 9, 11, 15, 17, 18
tunnels 11

underpass 19

walking bus 5
wildlife 7, 9, 16